A Product of the System

Corey Titus

LOST MEMORIES ARE LIKE PICTURES FALLING OUT OF YOUR BACKPACK, SCATTERED IN THE WIND.

CONTENTS

Introduction

It's funny the things you remember, what memories stand out when you are older. Although I don't vividly remember much about my first experience in foster care because I was so young, the thing that stands out for me is the yellow jeep the case worker was driving. I wasn't even in school yet, I was about 3. My brother Brandon had gone to school covered in bruises from our Dad's latest episode with the bottle, and the school called CPS. Our Dad was a mean drunk, and my siblings and I took the brunt of his abuse. I was in about nine different placements throughout my childhood; foster homes, group homes, and even a psych ward when they couldn't find anywhere else to put me because I kept running away. Some of these places I didn't really mind, hell I even liked a couple of them, but all I ever wanted to do was go home to my Mom and my sister. That's all a kid really wants, a safe place with a family that they love and love them back. I wonder what older me would have told younger me in that moment when I was being driven away in the bright yellow Jeep, would there have been anything that would have actually helped at that moment?

In one of the foster homes I was in, the Mom would ask me questions about my life, and she would always tell me, "you are going to write a book." She gave me a notebook and tried to encourage me to write, but at the time I thought, no way you are just trying to make money off of me. Now that some time has passed, all I want is to get these words down, get these memories out of my head and onto paper, to show people what it is really like growing up in the system. This book is half a healing exercise, and half a call to action because there are still so many kids still in the system that deserve better than I got.

CH. 1

That first placement, I was placed with my Brother at a boy's home, and I remember it was right before Christmas. I remember the fire department came with a fake Santa for all of the kids. I had gotten a Gameboy with Pokémon games, and I loved that thing. The older boys stole my Gameboy and hid it in the ceiling tiles, but the staff found it. There was a big building with lots of rooms, and each room had bunk beds. There was a huge gym shower, with three shower heads on each wall. When I was taking a shower in there, I slipped and split my chin open. I ran out naked and crying, getting blood everywhere. It was so bad I had to get stitches, and they gave me a huge Bob the Builder lollipop to make me feel better, one of those fancy soft ones. Like I said, it's funny what you remember.

From there I went to a nice family. They had this nice big house, with a guest house on the property, and they hid all the gifts around for us to find. I don't know how long I was there, but I do remember them having twin girls. One day the girls asked me if I would want to be adopted. All I said was that I miss my mom. I would cry and ask when my mom was going to come to get me. Everything revolved around me seeing my mom and my grandparents. I wanted to get to them and out of this house, it didn't matter how nice they were, I wanted my family. I was too young to really understand what was going on, but looking back I wish that I had stayed with that family. Once when I went back to CPS I asked the caseworker at that point if they could place me with them again, but they said they couldn't. I assumed that they had adopted someone else and didn't have room for me anymore. Even to this day, I wonder what would have been if I had just stayed with that family. My grandparents spent a lot on lawyers to get me back to my Mom, and all the time I heard them saying that they spent over 70 thousand on lawyers, and Mom kept losing us to CPS over and over.

After our grandparents got us out of CPS, my Mom didn't want us, so she dropped us off with my Dad. My grandma and her boyfriend, who was a complete asshole, lived there. My grandma collected antiques, then she would sell them. She was really into stuff like Felix the cat, Pink Panther, Tom and Jerry. They had a three-bedroom house, one was decorated with Felix, one was decorated with patch dolls, and the last one was our Grandma's bedroom. Her boyfriend Chet slept on the couch. Everything was cheetah print in that house, or leopard prints, any kind of cat prints really. Although she let us stay with them, we didn't get to have one of the bedrooms, they were for her things. I can't imagine having the extra room and not letting little kids use it.

When I lived with my Dad, we had to stay in the garage, and the conditions were seriously deplorable. Dad stayed in the garage with us. We had bunk beds, a queen-size on the bottom, double on top. There were two couches, a tv, and a turtle tank. Dad kept his drum set in the center of the room and he would play when he got drunk. There was a washing machine and dryer, and a deep freezer in the garage as well. We didn't have a dresser or a closet, so there were tubs of clothes everywhere. The garage was never transferred from its original state, it wasn't like they turned it into an extra space in the home, it was just a garage. In order to keep bugs out, we had newspapers lined on the bottom and around cracks. I remember the garage door being off the hinge, so half of the top was open still. In the winter we would freeze, and summer was so hot. You could not walk around barefoot, or even see the floor, because of dirt and clothes and just trash everywhere. There were lots of rats and roaches, and I was (still am) scared of rats, so I couldn't sleep because I would see rats running across the room. I'd have to stomp at the rats to make them run away so we could walk past.

I'd go to school smelly a lot, I remember my feet stinking

so bad I threw away my shoes because I was embarrassed to wear them. The kids would make fun of me for the smell. My Dad beat my ass for throwing away the shoes, he thought I threw them away because I was trying to get out of going to school. After that he made me go to school with his shoes, his big ass shoes on my little feet, grass stains and everything. He put them on extra tight, and I remember the teacher looking at me confused, but she didn't ask me why I was wearing those shoes. I was bullied for my stinky feet in elementary school, I remember a kid dared me to lick the bottom of the shoe, and at the time it didn't seem that nasty to me, kids are gross. I licked the bottom of the shoe, and everyone was laughing at me. I thought they were laughing with me, I guess that is my defense mechanism, to turn anything that makes me uncomfortable into a joke, or laugh it off.

Even normal things, like having pets, were strange for us growing up. Living in the garage with Dad, he and his friend Peter found baby raccoons in a dumpster at an apartment complex, two of them that we named Bonnie and Clyde. We would feed them honey pops cereal, and we would let them crawl on us when they were little. Once they got older they started to hiss and scratch, so we had to get rid of them. One time I went to the corner store with Dad and he had the raccoon on his shoulder, but when they saw him they locked the doors and wouldn't let us in. I was laughing because the raccoon had diarrhea all down his back. We loved those raccoons when they were little. My Grandma had a pet pig in the backyard for a while, and it would always get stuck in the crack where the inground pool wasn't filled in on the sides with concrete. We would feed the pig leftovers from dinner, but it eventually died. The strangest story though was when we had a big beehive on the side of the house, and the bees stung our dog to death. That was so crazy it was actually on the news.

Dad also had us doing shady shit with him all the time. One night around 10, my Dad woke me up, "hey come on you are going to help me." Then he gives me a backpack with wire cutters and bolt cutters in it. There was a new subdivision being built by this forest area, and they already had the telephone poles set up. My Dad climbed up the pole and cut the power lines, and wrapped it up in a coil, a big bunch of it. We drove to Conroe a couple days later, we threw all the power lines in a hole to burn off the outside, and in the morning we were left with only the copper. We took them to the scrap yard for money. We did things like this a lot, they would say "let's go scrapping", and we would go with whoever had a truck. We went through people's trash, cutting cords, getting the copper and metal out of it, and taking it to the scrap yard for cash.

When we were living with Dad, I saw my older brother get jumped by these guys that lived three houses down from us. I ran out of the garage with a hockey stick in my hands, but I was too scared to help because they were teenagers and I was just a little kid. This guy blew his cigarette smoke in Brandon's face outside, and Brandon was yelling at him, "come on, step into the yard I'll beat your ass." Brandon pulled the cigarette out of the guy's mouth and put it in the guy's face. All three of the guys jumped Brandon, pulled him out into the street, and started stomping on him. I ran into the house and told my Dad that Brandon was getting jumped, so Dad grabbed his gun and ran outside. The other guy's Dad was out there too though, so the two Dads squared off about to fight too. My Dad pulls his shirt up to show off his gun, but the other guy's dad already had his gun in his hand at this point. Brandon got up off the street with a bloody nose. One of the other guys had his shirt ripped off, with huge scratches down his back, face, and chest. It was such a crazy day, and a really intense experience for me because after that I had to pass their house when I would walk to and from school and they would taunt me as I went by.

Drama, violence, and hate were normal for me growing up. My Dad tried to force racism on me at a young age, he was really big into the KKK and white power stuff. He bought me a big Popeye, the sailor man coloring book, and would make me draw black people hanging on the apple tree, or being drug behind a truck, tied up with ropes. I had to draw swastikas all over the book, and if I didn't draw it correctly, he would throw beer bottles at the wall near my head, or make me drink the whiskey he had. I still remember how that shit would burn my chest. Once I learned how to draw the swastika correctly, he took cigarette askes and ink from a pen, and mixed it all up with toothpaste in a bowl. He gave me a box cutter blade and had me cut the swastika into his leg, on his calf. Once it was done, he put my hand in the bowl of mixed-up ink and told me to rub it into the cut. Every time it scabbed up, he would peel it off, to the point that it left a scar like a tattoo. It looks like shit but he was proud of it. I didn't want to be racist because I didn't want to be like him. What a cruel thing, to try and poison a child like that. In a way, the system saved me because I would have been screwed up if I would have had to grow up with my parents. My dad was actually successful at one point, he had a pool company, but those brown bottles of liquor overtook him and made him into a different man, a man I didn't want to be around. He definitely was not a man that I wanted to be like.

CH. 2

That first experience traumatized me, my sister Kimberly just disappeared, my brother Brandon disappeared, and I was left all alone. I was young and confused, and no one was telling me anything that I could understand. I was just sitting in a room with a bean bag and toys, waiting by myself. I wanted to get up and do something, but I didn't know what. I didn't know where I was about to go, or what's going to happen. I remember the feeling of being so lost, scared, and anxious. Everything was a big question mark. They brought me snacks and a bag with some clothes that didn't fit me, and also a blanket. I couldn't really eat because I was too nervous, my stomach was in knots.

During some visits to the CPS offices, I would go wandering around the building, and another case worker would spot me. Saying "Who is this little kid just wandering around?" Sometimes I would sneak into their fridge to see what they had. They would find me and tell me I couldn't be in there and bring me back to the cps visiting area. I wasn't trying to be bad, I just wanted to run around, I just wanted to get out of that room. I was a bored kid just trying to find something to do. Sometimes I would like to sit and just look out the window. I would try to eavesdrop on the workers, trying to find out what they were talking about, were they talking about my mom. Any word that I could make out seemed important, it was a piece of information at least. I wanted so badly to know what they were saying, what was going to happen to me next.

Every time they would walk me through a parking garage, up some stairs, or into a big building, I would think "oh shit am I in another CPS building." There was a file room right when you walked into the hall that had a big wall of files, and those were all of the kids that they were managing. They would say "Which one are you" and they find your file, "oh here he is." I wondered how long they had those records, just a wall of kids' lives in this room. It made me feel lost, overwhelmed with the size of what that number must be, the number of kids just like me. Leaving a nervous feeling in my stomach, especially if Kimberly wasn't with me. If I couldn't be with my Mom, I at least wanted to be with Kimberly. She was my anchor, my tie to my family, the one person I could talk to about anything.

CPS visits with my Mom or grandparents were sitting in

that file room, sometimes with gift bags and balloons, I would always try to peek around that corner as we walked up, hoping to see my family waiting for me there. Dad didn't show up to a lot of visits because he lived so far away, and eventually he lost his license after a DUI. If they don't show up to the visits, I would just sit in that room with Kimberly crying, left with that feeling of shattered expectation. That room ended up meaning so much to me. One of my foster moms would ask me "why are you crying, they don't want you, they aren't here and they know you are here." How could you say that to a child experiencing such profound heartbreak?

A lot of the visits would be just me and Kimberly. Sometimes we would see our Mom, but if she didn't show, at least I would see my sister. Mom would make promises all of the time, saying that she would be there, but most of the time she wouldn't show up. One day I was crying on the phone because I wanted to see her so badly, and it was that moment that I realized you can't beg someone to love you. It's no surprise that so many kids from the foster system end up with drug problems or issues with getting in trouble. How are you supposed to deal with the feeling of being lost and alone, knowing that there was no one there for you? There is no way to describe what it feels like, the abandonment, the sense of how unjust and unfair it all is. You cry, you rage, you run away, and you make bad decisions because there is no one there to help you make good ones.

CH. 3

Looking back on the time I spent living with my Dad, I realize that I didn't always recognize how crazy the situation was while it was happening. When you are a kid, all you know is your own situation, and that is what is normal for you. If you have always lived your life in the dark, you don't know what the light is. Of course, during the really violent moments, I knew then and there that this was fucked up. Other times though, through the eyes of a child, it seemed like a wild adventure. This became a theme for that part of my childhood, there was a kind of dichotomy, which version of my father would I be getting that day? And even if I didn't get the best version of him, would it still be better than the worst? It was like living with Dr. Jekyll and Mr. Hyde.

There was one time, standing in the kitchen, a can of unopened green beans went flying across the room, everything went into slow motion and shit got dark real fast. At that moment I was sorry for telling my drunk dad that I didn't want "no fucking peanut butter and bananas in my pasta." When the can hit me and split my fingers, my first reaction was to run to the bathroom and get a towel to try and put pressure on it. Unfortunately, in the process of me running out of the room, I knocked over the pot of noodles, burning the shit out of my bleeding hand. My Grandma came in to see why there was so much noise, and she found her kitchen counters covered in my blood. At that moment my Dad realized that he had fucked up and rushed over to try and help me. I never got stitches on my hand, but the cuts were really deep and I still have the scars. Whenever I see these scars, all I think about is my dad, and I'm actually glad I have them because as bad as it might sound, it's all I have from him to go along with these stories.

On my tenth birthday, I was walking with my dad, who was of course drunk, to the corner store to buy more beer. He was twirling his drumsticks around his fingers the entire walk there and back because he always played the drums when he was drunk. As we were walking back from the store, I was hit by a car as we were crossing the street. I rolled up the hood, and when they braked, I flew off the hood and went sliding on the concrete. Holding onto my ribs, I looked up and saw my Dad smashing the windshield of the car with his drumsticks. The person who hit me then pressed on the gas and shot out of there with only a broken windshield. I thankfully didn't have any broken bones, just some scratches, and bruises. When we got home, I went to the garage and started to play Grand Theft Auto, killing the cops and ambulance workers in the game. The crazy part was that the real cops had been called about the incident, and they had come to check on me. So, imagine them standing there asking me questions, the whole while I'm just playing this game, killing these cops on the screen and telling the real ones, "This will be you," thinking it was funny. What a sick thing to say to them when they were just trying to help me, it really gives you some perspective on the mindset I was being raised in.

My dad taught me how to swim by holding me down under the water, he would spin me around, then take me up for a quick breath of air. The lesson was you better take that opportunity for a breath when you can. I learned how to swim just to get away from him. That was one of the reasons I was scared of him, shit like that. I can remember coughing up water. But it's funny that even the bad memories with my dad are good ones now looking back. It's like I would take almost anything, put up with almost anything, just not to be taken away again. Dad would get drunk and throw beer bottles at me as I would laugh and dodge them, better to laugh than be afraid I guess. One time my brother and I were playing the Simpsons video game, and Dad's friend came over, a big guy. Brandon said hi, he knew him, and then this guy sat down on the couch behind us and started smoking crack. Eventually, Dad comes home and he starts smoking too. He was so nice on crack, whatever I asked him for he was like sure. I remember thinking, man can you do this instead of the brown bottle?

There was a time when me and Kimberly were living with our Dad at our grandparents' house, in the garage, and CPS came by to do a home study. They said that we kids could stay there, but our Dad could not be in the house with us. So my Grandma Terry had my Dad living in her antique shop, and we would go visit him there while she was working. One time while he was living out there, Dad had bought a mini crotch rocket, and Kimberly was driving that thing around the storage unit parking lot. Somehow she crashed into a brick wall going pretty fast. She was laying in a pool of her own blood, and someone stopped to help her. I didn't find out what happened until she was already on her way to the hospital. She had a fractured skull and was unconscious for a few days, or a week, I don't remember. It was really scary, but I had a gut feeling that she was going to be ok. She was covered with bruises, he was really traumatized from the bike accident, who wouldn't be?

There was another time my Dad was walking me and Kimberly to the park, I was in third or fourth grade, and Kimberly was in the 5th. This kid named Alex used to bully me all the time, and he was at the park in the neighborhood. I was being annoying and talking a lot, and my Dad told the kid "I'll give you 10 bucks if you beat Corey's ass." My dad didn't know that this was the kid that had been bullying me, but Kimberly knew, and before the kid could get off his bike I pushed him down and started beating on him. I remember how afterward Kimberly went bragging to all of her friends at school about how her brother beat up a 5th grader, and that made me proud, but really I was scared the entire time. There was another kid named Aberham on the school bus, who spit on my sister and called her a bitch. I punched him in his nose so hard I made it bleed and got kicked off for fighting. My Dad was mad because now I had to walk home from school. It was only like four blocks away from the house, but he was still mad. I didn't care, I wanted to prove to my sister that I would fight for her, that I would stick up for her. I never liked to fight, I never felt like it was me, but I needed her to know how much I loved her, and that I would always stick up for her.

CH. 4

My Grandma died of cancer, and her boyfriend Chet ended up getting everything. Chet treated us horribly, he was just an awful man. Chet would hit Kimberly with a dog leash, but he had Parkinson's, so his hand was always shaking. One time my Dad got into a fight with him over that and slammed him really hard into the counter. Chet went to his room and got a gun, and he aimed it at my dad. My Dad, this crazy ass, put the barrel of the gun into his mouth and said "Shoot me mother fucker." Chet's hand was shaking holding the gun, and you could hear the metal of the gun hitting my Dad's teeth. That sound is impossible to describe, it's one of the most terrifying noises you can imagine. Chet ended up not pulling the trigger, I think he was too freaked out, we all were really. That scene was just insane.

My Dad got arrested for spitting on a cop, and they took me in my underwear, they didn't even let me get dressed. They put me in the back of the cop car like that. They gave me a blanket in the car, and I got clothes when I got to the placement center. At the time everything was so crazy I didn't really think about it, but looking back that seems so odd. Why couldn't they at least let me grab clothes to get dressed in the back of the car? I don't know why Brandon didn't come with us, why he was allowed to stay. The next day my Dad's Mom, Grandma Terry, came and picked me and Kimberly up from Chimney Rock, which was a holding place for CPS kids, and we went back home to our garage. I remember Chet being mad that we were back. After that, Chet kicked us out and we went to stay with Brad Boyd, who was like a godfather to us. He lived with his parents, so we only stayed for three days. Then he dropped us off with Johnny, my Mom's old boyfriend for a few months. I really loved Brad, sometimes he would take us to church or out to eat, and he even bought us clothes. Dad and Brad fell out because my Dad never paid him back for anything that he did for us. I always wanted to tell him thank you for everything that he did.

I really liked staying with Johnny, they had a big excavator in the back of the property, and he had a friend that left his truck out in the back of his property for too long. For my birthday he let me dig a big hole, and I knocked the truck into it and smashed it up. I had the best time. This guy comes back weeks later, and Johnny said "I told you to get that shit weeks ago", then he sees his truck in the hole all smashed up. Johnny had dirt bikes we would ride to the corner store, I'd ride the mini one. He was with another woman then named Sandy, and I remember she had some kind of birth defect with her hand, her knuckles were really swollen and her fingers were curved in. She was always nice, but she would get into arguments with Kimberly. I was in 4th grade, and Kimberly was in the 5th at this point. We eventually got dropped at our grandparents' house, because my Dad was getting out of jail soon. Dad knew about my Mom and Johnny, but they never had beef, he kinda didn't care. We stayed with my grandparents for a couple weeks, then went to stay with Shannon. I didn't like staying there, I had to sleep on a giant pile of clothes.

My Dad was in jail for about two months. When he got out, he started treating us really well after that. I think the loss of family kind of put things in perspective for him. That didn't last forever, of course, one day he got drunk again and hit Kimberly. The cops came to investigate and he spit on one of the officers, so that is when they put him in jail. CPS came and took us to a pre-placement, which was just a big room with a lot of cots, a tv, and a washer and dryer. You couldn't leave that room until someone came to get you, and there was always a worker sitting at the door in a chair making sure we didn't go anywhere. I remember an older kid ran away, and that was the first time it occurred to me, damn you can run away? It was like a lightbulb went off over my head, the idea of running away gave me a sense of power, of control over a situation I had no control over.

CH. 5

When I got back with mom, she never had a job that I could remember, though I know that she did security at the airport at one time. When she was at work she was going down an escalator, and she broke her knee. That's when she got addicted to the pain meds that they gave her. I would cry every time she left because I knew she wouldn't be back for weeks, she would leave in her uniform like she was going to work, but just wouldn't come back. Mom would leave us for weeks or months at a time. She would go smoke, live her wild life, whatever she wanted to do. She would eventually show back up and ask her parents for money, and they would always give it to her. Mom had a brother who died from a heroin overdose before I was born, he overdosed in their house. I think that is why they were so lenient with her, why they gave her anything she wanted. They knew she was on drugs, but they loved her and spoiled her big time. They would watch Dr. Phil and Cops, and they would say "oh that guy is a crackhead", and all the while I'm thinking, yeah my Mom is too. Her parents always gave her money, they were well off, and they gave her money all the time. They bought her cars, she totaled them, so they bought her another. It was a repeating cycle.

My grandparents had a condo in Galveston but only lived there three months out of the year. At this point, my Mom had a boyfriend named Benny, and they would stay at their place while they were gone. One time they went to a Uhaul place to grab something, and Kimberly and I were on the back of the truck. We told Benny to slow down, but he sped up instead hitting the speed bumps causing us to fall off. We got a terrible road rash all over us. It was so painful that we were out of school for a week. Most of the time when mom left us, she went to stay with Benny. He played the guitar at a bar, I remember he would play Stevie Ray Vaughn covers, and sometimes she would take us to listen. I remember one time he dropped me off a Snoopy coloring book for my birthday. Another time he took me to a Halloween party where we bobbed for apples, and he tried to get me to eat a worm. He told me I would live longer, but I said no, there was no way I was stupid enough to fall for that. Mom was with him for years, then he ended up going away to a mental hospital because he was schizophrenic. One time I heard him crying on the phone with my Mom at the mental hospital because he didn't have his Charmin toilet paper.

My grandparents did put Mom in jail once when my Mom

pushed her Dad down the stairs. That finally crossed a line and they actually called the cops on her. This was once I was an adult, not when we were kids. She was in for six or nine months, and she would get care packages sent to her. Then they called me and spent hundreds of dollars so that I could bond her out. I guess they were starting to feel guilty after some time had passed, they always forgave her, even when they probably shouldn't have. They spent 5 grand on a lawyer to get her out, and then she was free to make the same mistakes she had always been making. If you never make someone live with the consequences of their actions, they never have a reason to change.

When my grandparents passed, they left her houses and money. She tore up the houses, there was shit and condoms all over the floor. It didn't matter, she had money and she smoked it all away. When the money started to run out she had to sell the houses, but she had messed them up so badly that she had to sell them for super cheap. For a good three years, she smoked crack in fancy hotel rooms, not having to worry about anything, just living the life she wanted to live. She could have kept one of the homes, had a stable place to live, saved a little of the money she inherited and had a normal life. But that's not what she wanted to do, that wasn't where her priorities were. My grandparents also owned a room at the Victorian, and when they died it was left to her and her brother. She never took care of her responsibilities with it though, so her

21

brother eventually kicked her out. Imagine having all of that handed to you and just wasting it all like that.

CH. 6

My grandparents hated it so much that my Mom always left me and Kimberly with them when she disappeared. It got to a point where my grandparents didn't want us there because they knew she was going to slip out the door unannounced. There would be times when we would live with our older sister Shannon in her 1 bedroom apartment, sleeping on the floor or couch or a pile of clothes. She had a mountain of clothes in the corner of the room that I would always sleep on. Mom would disappear, off to smoke crack, and Shannon would cuss her out for leaving me and Kimberly with her. Crack would be more important than me and Kimberly eating. I remember one of her drug dealers liked me, he always called me Dennis the Menace. He was a Hispanic guy with long black hair in a ponytail, he went by the name "BLUE", that's what everyone called him. He would always give me a TV dinner every time my mom would buy drugs from him, it almost became a routine where this guy was feeding me more than anyone else was. My mom would always live in apartments with Shannon, and her crackhead friends and Shannon's gangster friends would always be hanging out there. I remember stepping over a lot of beanie babies all over the floor, because either my sister Shannon or my mom collected them. The place was always really messy and dirty. Some of the craziest things that happened in Shannon's apartment are some of my worst memories.

Around the second grade, my mom was taking me back to my Dad's. Shannon never wanted me to be there because I was a mama's boy, but I just wanted to be with my mom. My Dad wanted me, but I didn't want to go there back to the beating and the rats. I didn't want to go, I was scared to go back. My mom was driving, and I was in the back seat, I jumped out and ran across the intersection. Shannon caught me and was holding me down in her lap so that I wouldn't get away. I managed to grab the handle of the car, trying to jump out while the car was moving. I was so close to the concrete. When we got to my Dad's, I wouldn't get out, so Shannon had to pull me out. She pushed me down and ran to my mom who had already driven a little bit away, she ran and jumped in the car. My dad had watched it all happen and just told me to come on in. My grandma would always tell me, "they don't want you", and my heart would break a little more each time because deep down I knew that she was right.

Another time I was at Shannon's apartment, I knew my Mom was going to go smoke, so I chased after her and grabbed the handle of the car, but she pulled off dragging me with her. I was bleeding and crying. Some people saw me and asked me where my family was. She didn't come back for a couple weeks. Every time she left I knew I wouldn't see her for a while. One of the scariest moments for me happened at that apartment. My Mom was on the ground and wouldn't wake up, something happened with the drugs she was taking, she was turning purple. Shannon told me to shut up because I was being too loud, I was freaking out, but Shannon kept saying she's fine. Shannon kept threatening to make me pass out if I didn't shut up. This is something that she would do to us, hold our nose and mouth until we passed out, she did it to me at least twice. This time I bit her to get away, I ran around trying to get out, and Kimberly and I ran out the window. The cops came that day, but they took Shannon's word over ours because she was an adult. Mom woke up but hid in the restroom. After that whole scene, we went to stay at a hotel.

There wasn't a tv or much entertainment, so me and Kimberly would be outside a lot playing with the other kids in the apartments. I remember a time when Shannon's friend was sleeping on the floor and he left his gun lying next to him, so I started playing with his loaded gun. I knew it was real and a part of me was scared, so when I was playing with it I wouldn't touch the trigger. I remember it being really heavy. The guy woke up and quickly snatched it from me. There were multiple times when I saw Shannon run to the restroom to flush drugs down the toilet because the cops were knocking on the door. Our apartment was always loud and a disturbance to the neighbors, so they got called a lot. My mom eventually would drop me and Kimberly off at our Dads telling him that she didn't want us.

As bad as things got, my Dad never abandoned us, that is one wound he never inflicted. He would make sure we ate well, we would play video games and watch movies, and things were mostly okay. But as soon as he picked up that cheap brand of whiskey, and started to drink it like it was water, he would turn into a completely different person. I truly believe if my dad wasn't a drunk that he would have been a good guy, but that brown bottle took over his mind and made him abusive and scary. I remember the last cps visit I had with my dad, it was me Kimberly and my Dad was crying when I walked in. He told us, "I love y'all, but I won't be able to see y'all anymore, they are taking my rights away." When he told me that I felt like a piece of me was missing, me and Kimberly began to cry, and the rest of the visit was just us crying together. I feel like that was more traumatizing than having beer bottles thrown at me, or getting hit with a drumstick, just knowing that I would rather deal with my Dad's alcohol problems than go back to a foster home. I felt anxious, lost, and scared, I was so hurt.

CH. 7

My mom wasn't just a crackhead or a pill head, she dealt
out her fair share of abuse too. Mom would take her car
keys and stab me in the back, or scratch me with them on
the side of my ribs, and it actually hurt more than Dad's
drumstick. She would threaten me and Kimberly, saying
she would drop us off at our Dads and leave us there. It
was really Shannon pushing for that because Shannon
didn't want us in her apartment. Having kids around got in
the way when all you wanted to do was party. Kids need
attention, and food, they require time. Me and Kimberly
were jealous of Shannon because she was hogging our
mom. She got to keep a relationship with her, even if it was
an unhealthy one. Mom had such little patience with us, we
would just be behaving like silly kids, acting up, and she
would lash out at us. One time we were walking into a
Walmart, and I told Kimberly "hey watch this", and I
started acting like I had mental health problems, like
walking with a limp and dragging my foot, just mumbling
really loud and banging my arm on my chest. Kimberly was
laughing so hard at me, and then boom car keys straight to
the gut. I was just trying to make Kimberly laugh and
embarrass my mom at the same time, mission

accomplished, but that car key was no joke.

A lot of trips to Walmart consisted of me and Kimberly going to the bakery and getting food, then we would walk around Walmart eating stuff that we didn't pay for, and just leave while our mom stole stuff so she could return it at another Walmart. Mom would tell me and Kimberly to steal stuff all the time. I used to steal DVDs or take the cd out of the case, then watch them at my grandparents' house. I think about it now like man that's so wrong, but at the time it was almost like a competition between me and Kimberly who would come out of Walmart with the best stuff. I would usually win because I'm really competitive. Kimberly was caught a couple times, and I was almost caught one time running out of Academy with a pair of Heelys on my feet, those shoes with the wheel on the bottom. I remember begging my mom to buy them for me, I told her if u can't buy them then let me go in and get them. She waited in the van and I jumped in with the tags and everything, the alarm at the door going off. It was so funny getting into my Mom's van and just pulling out all this stuff from my pockets and underwear, just so much candy and toys and DVDs. I distinctly remember The Cat in the Hat DVD in particular. Our Mom would encourage that kind of activity, while our Dad would beat our asses for stealing and make us go back in the store and apologize. He would tell us "I'm going to cut off your hands if you keep stealing, just like they did in the old days", he was just joking, but we understood the point he was making. Once I got to cps all that stealing stuff stopped because I wasn't interested in it didn't involve the competition with Kimberly.

I would occasionally ask my Mom for things when I wasn't with her. One time I got her to buy me blue Beats headphones, and at the time it was a big deal for me because it was something that I always wanted, and I was so happy that she got them for me. It turns out that she used the money she was stealing from my aunt who had dementia. I thought about it, like damn she was stealing from a lady with dementia to get me something I wanted, that was so nice of her in a really messed up way. My sister Shannon ended up pawning them to pay her phone bill, she told me she would get them out of the pawn shop, but she never did get them back for me. I'm still a little salty about it because it had some sentimental value behind it, my Mom actually once got me something that I really wanted. When you are craving a connection with a parent, you will latch onto anything. I was once at a cps meeting, asking my mom for pictures of her and she brought me a card then, it played the song "Everybody wants to rule the world." And I kept playing it over and over. I thought that my mom was trying to tell me something, that I couldn't have what I wanted because I wanted her. One of the kids in the room with me told me to shut up because he didn't want to hear it anymore.

My mom would always get paranoid when she smoked, thinking people were following us, swerving the car. This obviously created a very dangerous situation. When I was twelve my mom got into a huge car accident, the car flipped about 20 times. A black Chevy Silverado hit us at his driver-side headlight, we were going 55/60, and we flipped over him, the angle was just right. There was zero damage to his truck, but we just kept flipping, my head kept hitting the ceiling of the car. The back was all smashed in, and twisted metal cut me on the back of my head. A cop just happened to be there and saw the whole thing, which ended up being a good thing because he could call for help right away. We had just left my Mom's parents' house to get money to 'fix the brakes', but she was really going to get smoke. She was using the emergency brake as the brakes because they didn't work. Shannon flew out of the open sunroof, she wasn't wearing her seat belt, how she only got a broken wrist and scratches I will never understand, she could have died. Kimberly threw herself over Xavier's (Shannon's kid) car seat to protect him. Her back got all cut up from the flying glass, and I got hit in the head so I was all cut up, I still have a bump on the back of my head. I wasn't wearing a seat belt, I was holding onto the handles of the door.

There was a woman who was trying to take care of me and make me sit down. I thought that I was going to die. I kept asking the lady if I was okay, there was blood on my hands, on my neck. I kept trying to walk around, to see what was happening. She was trying to get me to sit down, I remember my hands shaking. She gave me her phone to use, I called my grandma, crying sitting on the road. They were shocked, what are you talking about, you just left here! They didn't even come to the accident, the ambulance was already there. I thought my mom was going to die, the way she was screaming in pain, and humped over in the front. My mom was stuck in the car, the gas pedal got stuck between her toes, and busted her foot all up. They had to use the jaws of life to get her out. I didn't even see Shannon, she was on the other side of the street. Kimberly got out of the car, holding the car seat, crying. At that moment I was so scared. The inside of my chest was shaking, I didn't know it could do that, pure panic. I had my PlayStation with me in the car, the slim silver one, the new model my Dad had bought for me, was in the front seat pocket, and slammed into my forehead. I never saw it after, which was salt in the wound. When I was in the ambulance on the way to the hospital I was so sleepy, they kept saying don't fall asleep, don't fall asleep. When I was released I had a neck brace on, I was covered in bruises from being thrown around, and my head was a mess. All things considered, we fared well, somehow Xavier only had one little cut on his nose. Lesson learned, always wear your seatbelt. When we left the hospital at about one am, we took a cab to Shannon's apt. We all took turns soaking in Epsom salt in the bath, and I remember my water turned orange from all of the dried blood on my body. Trying to sleep on that pile of clothes, because I didn't have a bed there, was the most uncomfortable thing ever. Kimberly had a huge purple bruise on her leg, it was so painful for her.

CH. 8

Not too long after that, Shannon was smoking weed, they were kinda getting Kimberly on weed at the time. For some reason they weren't passing it to her, so she went and got a fire extinguisher and sprayed them since they were not sharing. In that same span of time, me and Kimberly weren't going to school, we just refused to go, and that was why the truancy officers eventually came. A few months went by and that's when the girls got into a huge fight. Kimberly pushed Shannon out of the window, her ass was sticking out of the window where it broke, but she didn't fall out. The truancy officers just happened to show up on the same day as the cops did because we had missed so much school, but somehow we didn't end up leaving with either of them. Me and Kimberly left with mom to stay at her parents' house, then a CPS worker told mom that we had to go and talk to them at the main building. We all did separate interviews, when they took Kimberly it made me nervous, then they took Brandon and I started crying because I didn't want to be alone. I told them I wanted Brandon, but she said that he left with your mom already. I asked her where Kimberly was. They told me that she had already been placed with another family and that they were going to find one for me too. I was heartbroken, and scared, and did the only thing I could think of. I ran out of the front door, out of the parking garage, and then ran into a store. I asked to use the phone, but the lady was curious why I wasn't with an adult, I mean I was just a kid. I called my mom, and I was trying to tell her where I was, so I handed the phone to the lady so she could give the address to my mom. I waited and waited but my mom never came. I got freaked out and ran out of that store too.

I ran into a restaurant, and the employees stopped me and gave me an orange juice and a cookie. I was crying and scared, and I just wanted my mom to come and get me. I saw a taxi, so I ran over to it crying and asked for a ride, of course, the guy said no I can't just give a kid a ride. I went back into the restaurant, where the case worker came and got me, then she took me to my first foster home in Pearland. Terry Barnes was the mom's name, she had about 8 kids in the home. I was so scared going in. I remember that they were watching this comedian Gabriel Iglesias, and it made me dislike him because they were having a good time. They were laughing, making fried chicken, and I hated that they could be happy when I was so sad. I just laid on the bunk bed crying. Eventually, another of the foster brothers came in to calm me down, he told me "it's ok you don't have to cry." He was trying to be kind, but I knew right then that I was going to run away.

They took me to the area of town that I was from to go shopping for clothes, I snuck out and went to the grocery store next door, then I ran out of there and started running down the freeway. I ran for over 45 minutes until I got to the mall. A woman stopped to offer me a ride, and I thought she looked familiar. It turns out it was a lady who went to church with Brad Boyd, the friend of my Dads who would take me and Kimberly to church and buy us nice clothes for school, so I met her when I used to go with him. I ran away from her because I saw her work badges, and I knew that she would turn me in. I made it to Shannon's apartment, but no one was there, it had been empty for days. I stayed there for about a day and a half before my friend's mom called cps on me, and told them where I was hiding. I didn't want to go back to the foster home, so I went down to the payphone by the pool and called my mom. She was staying with a guy, sleeping with him in exchange for crack. I would just watch movies for hours while they got high and had sex. After a little while, I went to my mom's parents' house for a couple days before I went to cps again. My grandparents knew that I was supposed to be in CPS, and they were scared that the cops would show up and they would get into trouble, so they told me that I couldn't stay there. I went to the park in the neighborhood just one more time before I went back to CPS. Almost every time I would go back to cps it was me either walking into the cps building or just calling the cops and telling them that I ran away. Occasionally someone would see a little kid walking alone and ask me if I was okay, and I'd tell them "well I ran away from CPS" straight up.

CH. 9

They placed me at a 90-day shelter called Lamar village, Kimberly was also at this shelter, so I actually got to see her. This was the first time Kimberly and I were placed together, so that was a big deal being able to see her so much. It was a big property, with two houses in the front, and two in the back. The back houses were where we slept, one for girls and one for boys, and the front was administrative. The front property also had a few rooms, and they gave them to the kids that were about to leave the facility. I felt like they might have kept the bad kids there too because there was a lot more staff in the front. There were also a few 17-year-olds there too who were about to age out of the system. There was a kitchen in the front house where they would cook all the food, then they had a van that would bring it to the back houses for the kids. The food wasn't bad, nothing too exciting, but nothing stood out that I really disliked. There were always two big pitchers with saran wrap over the top that had kool-aid made with way too much sugar, so I had to water it down to drink it. The other kids would push the saran wrap into the kool-aid, which was annoying. The food would always come in aluminum trays, with paper plates, paper cups, and plastic silverware. Every morning they had cinnamon pop tarts, but they didn't put them in the toaster, they put them on heating trays to warm them up. They were good but it was the same thing every day. If the other kids didn't want them I would take them to school and eat them throughout the day.

They moved my room around a lot because I wasn't getting along with the other kids. Honestly, this wasn't my fault, you put enough young boys together and shit is going to happen. I got into a fight with a kid named Mason. I was on the bottom bunk, and he was shaking the bed because he was jacking off. I pulled him off the top bunk and started hitting him. The worker agreed with me that he shouldn't be doing that, so they let me sleep on the couch until I moved to a different room. At one point I shared a room with a kid named Brandon, but I got into a fight so had to move again. There were six rooms in this big old house, with two bunk beds in each room. We had about 13 to 16 boys in the house. The kitchen was empty because they would bring the food in, I think this was to keep us from sneaking food in the middle of the night. The living area had wood floors, but there was really thin carpet throughout the rest of the place. The bathrooms were really dirty, and we rotated doing the chores, but that's not ever going to work when you are talking about kids being in charge of cleaning. Especially having that many boys using the same bathrooms, it's going to be gross.

There was a really big field by the houses, and we would play football out there. That was the first time I was introduced to football, and it's something I still love. On the weekends the staff members would spend time with us. One staffer would bring his PlayStation 3, it was new then, and he would let us each play for 20-30 minutes so that we could all play. I would watch the other kids play and wait for my turn. One of the staff members took me and six of the boys in his truck back to his house, he had a side hustle selling bootleg movies, so he let us pick out what movies we wanted to watch, and we got to bring them back. These were movies that were still in the theater. His name was Byron, he was older with a black beard, and black hair with a small white patch of gray hair on the top of his head. He was really nice to us, he would sit and talk with you if you had any problems, he was a good guy. Sometimes we would go walking in the big field, and I would sit and talk to Kimberly. The guys would always try to flirt with Kimberly, so I was popular in my house because of her. The guys would try to impress her by looking after me. One guy Marvin had an Airforce One shoe collection, he had a cool gold pair, and he let me wear them to school. Everyone was staring, I felt like the shit. He did it to impress her, but I don't think they ever dated. He even let me play his PlayStation.

I was in the sixth grade, and Kimberly was in the seventh. This place ended up being one of my favorite placements. I actually enjoyed emergency shelters more than the foster homes. I was used to being in a mom's trap house, I was used to chaos and violence, and people coming and going. It was oddly reassuring, I needed that drama. I became friends with the staff members and heard about their drama. I was more friends with the staff than the other kids. Each week we would have therapy. They would tell me what my goals were for the week. I had long-term goals like stabilizing my behavior, getting closer to reunification, that kind of stuff. You are only there for 90 days, so you lose friends, but it's fun seeing who is coming next. At a foster home, you might get stuck with a jerk. It was more entertaining there, you see more, you get to talk to the staff members, there is more to do.

Sometimes we just sit and talk about our stories, and you meet so many different personalities. It would get competitive, who had it worst, who is the hardest guy in here. I heard some wild stuff. One guy said his mom was in a shootout with Swat, and then killed herself. I was the one making it funny, my mom's a crack head and my dad's a drunk. I took my cue from Eminem, he told you everything wrong with him already, so what else is there to say? So no one can say anything about me, I already said it. They couldn't use it against me. People used to say that my mom didn't love me, it hurt my feelings but I tried not to show it.

I cried a lot as a young kid, but in a place like that you have to learn how to deal with your feelings, so I chose humor.

Even though I liked it there, I got into a few fights. I was in three different fights there. One time I was fighting a kid named Brandon because he stole some money from me that my Dad had given me during a visit. He gave me $50, which was a lot of money, and the kid stole some of it from me. The fight started in the kitchen and traveled outside. I hit him and he got wobbly so I hit him again and he passed out. I was so scared, I thought I killed him. I got into another fight there with a kid named Damian. He was my age, we were playing football, I ran him over and he didn't like it. We were 11 but his older brother was 16, he beat me down pretty badly. This guy Marvin, who was trying to impress Kimberly, came and saved me, so then they started fighting. The other fight was with that guy Marvin who woke me up shaking the bed, it was broken up by the staff members.

Kimberly and I would ride the bus together, the bus ride was about 14 mins. Kimberly had friends on the bus but I was quiet. Sometimes Kiimberly would borrow cell phones to call our mom or dad. They would always be telling lies, "those bastards, I'm trying to get you out, I'm going to all the classes." My mom always told us lies, what she knew we wanted to hear. We would skip school sometimes, we skipped with a bunch of other kids and hung out at the park. We got lost in the woods for most of the day, we were worried that we would be in so much trouble. We found a fence and followed it until we found a gate, made it just in time to make the bus, and the principal pulled us off. They would do random pop-ups at the school, always unannounced, and that was the day we skipped.

Coincidentally, right next to the group home were some apartments where Shannon's boyfriend Cedric lived. That time when we ran away, we planned it. Kimberly snuck out at night, Marvin woke me up, and I jumped out the window. We ran through the woods and hit a fence, then we crossed over to the apartment complex. We got there and of course he was surprised, we told him that we had just run away, and asked him to take us to Shannon's place. He sent a text message to one of the staff members, we had no idea they were friends. We got into his Impala, he drove us to McDonalds and gave us $10 for food, and then the police pulled up. They took us back and made me sleep on the couch with a staff member watching so that I couldn't run again. They interviewed us to ask why we left, and we told them we just wanted to see our family. A few days later Kimberly ran out of days at the shelter and was placed in a foster home. I was there for a couple weeks by myself. I was depressed and crying a lot, losing her was always the hardest part.

CH. 10

I went to another foster home with Mrs. Jacob's. When I was there, there was another foster kid named Derek. He was so dirty that he would shit on the floor and play in it, piss on the floor in his room, it was disgusting. I had a lot of problems with him because he would try to come to my room and touch my stuff. I didn't want his grimy hands anywhere near me. There was another boy there too named Qualin who was 2 years older than me. Qualin thought I was bullying Derek, and we started fighting. We went down the stairs into the kitchen where the foster mom tried to break it up and couldn't. I ended up breaking my hand hitting him. The next day my hand was purple, another couple of days went by and they took me to the hospital. I had a boxer's hairline fracture on my hand and had to get a cast. I remember telling lies to the counselor a lot, just trying my hardest for them to remove me from the home, I would even tell them I'm going to run away if you don't move me. I didn't like it there because of the other foster kids, and because Eric would make me feel uncomfortable. There is a big age difference, and Eric would punk me, but I stood no chance in a fight so I never tried.

I had a visit with my Mom, and when she sees the broken hand, she goes off on the caseworker. "Why was my son put in a situation to get hurt?" My mom acted like she was concerned like she cared about me. She would bring me pictures and candy during our visits (the ones she showed up for), and she would tell me that everything would be ok. Now that I have access to my case records, I know she never even showed up for the court dates or drug tests. She wasn't trying to get us back, it was pretend. So, she was going off on them, and I was crying because it was the first time seeing my mom for a long time. Each visit was just me crying because I just wanted to be with her. I didn't care what her situation was, I just wanted to be with my mom no matter what her lifestyle was. People laying on the floor with guns were normal to me. I didn't care about any of that, I would have put up with anything to be with her, to be loved by her.

Once I left that foster home, they placed me in a house with a foster Dad, and it was the strangest experience I had in all of foster care. He was this African guy, and there were two other Mexican boys there already. I only stayed there for 2 days. Those boys came from a really bad situation, so they didn't realize how weird this guy was. He tried feeding me white rice with a spoon of peanut butter on it for all three meals of the day. I asked the other boys, "are you serious", but they were fine with it, at least they were being fed. I got up to leave, and the foster Dad asked me what I was doing. I told him that I was leaving, and he grabbed me by the neck to stop me. We were standing by the garage area, and a neighbor who was outside could see us. I'm sure he was thinking "why is that African man grabbing that little white boy like that." I guess I was feeling dramatic, so I played it up, I started saying "I don't know who this guy is." He let me go because the neighbors were looking. I just told him that I was going to leave, and he said no, that he would take me wherever I wanted to go. He tricked me and took me to a mental hospital, but honestly, I was okay with it. The two other boys were so confused why I was happy going to a mental hospital, but I knew it wasn't normal what that man was doing, and I would be treated better there.

They took my belt and shoelaces, and I realized damn it's like a jail. There were teenagers there watching tv, and there was a nurse there watching over everyone, but they were all spaced out. I actually became friends with one of the male nurses who worked there, he would bring me snacks and rent movies for me. One time we watched Horton Hears a Who, I don't know why I remember that, but it was fun. There was another kid there, about 16, but was built like a big man. He was having some kind of episode, they laid him on the floor and they injected him in his but cheek and he fell right to sleep. They called it "the booty juice." I was there for a couple weeks. I felt trapped, no sunlight, I couldn't go outside, I wanted to run away. I would talk to my caseworker and beg her to come to get me. The hospital told them "we can't keep him here longer, nothing is wrong with him". They did all these interviews with me in the mental hospital, to get an assessment, but I was just a sad and angry kid. She was trying to get me home, but I was a runaway risk so no one wanted me. They have ratings for kids, ABC for behavior, and I was a C so no one wanted that risk.

Things would have been so much better if I could have been with Kimberly more, she was really the only family I had, but they kept separating us. Me and Kimberly were only placed in 2 foster homes and 1 emergency shelter together, they also had us at a CPS holding place for children. They placed us there countless times, the longest we would stay there were about 2 or 3 days at a time. That place sucked big time. Every time me and Kimberly ran away it was always to go find our mom, or run to our sister Shannon's house. We would just be turned back to CPS the next day. We wanted to be around her so bad, but she just never wanted to be around us. We were kids, we just wanted a relationship with our mom. We really just wanted to be a family.

CH. 11

In one of the foster homes, I was with Kimberly over the course of a summer. The foster Mom Loraine forced religion on us. We went to church three times a week. We would go to boys and girls camp at church all day, all the kids did, she also had three other foster kids who were siblings. I even had to go to church on my birthday, and I was so upset about that. They had a nice cake, but I didn't want to be there and I told them it was the worst birthday ever. We ran away from that foster home, and left everything we had there, at eleven o'clock at night. We went by a Church's Chicken, and we made up a story that we were at a friend's house and got kicked out so that they would let us use the phone to call Shannon. The employee gave us a ride across town to drop us off. The guy had to go home and change, and there was a guy on his couch smoking weed, he offered me a hit off his bong. I was only in the 6th grade. I declined, I didn't want to mess with that. They offered us some orange juice, and we took that. At this point it was one in the morning, so I was exhausted and I fell asleep in the car. When we finally made it to

Shannon's, she told us that we couldn't stay there. We were runaways, and she had a baby at this point, so she didn't want the trouble. We went through all of that to get there, and it was for nothing.

One time I went to my sister Shannon's place when she was older, she had 4 kids with her husband Orin She worked at McDonalds, and "O" (was his nickname) he worked at waste management, so basically I was the babysitter. I spent four or five months there. I used to sleep on a couch that they found on the curb somewhere. The couch had bedbugs and they would bite the shit out of me. It really sucks, you can't get them off of you. Those things are impossible to get rid of. One time I was trying to help O bbq, and I dropped the meat on accident into the dirt. I was laughing, and he got mad, and he said "it's only funny because you didn't pay for this shit." I don't know why I thought it was so funny, it really was an accident, but I felt bad afterward. I was just being a kid, but they didn't have any patience for that.

I remember this one foster home, Mr. and Mrs. Smith: They were really old, like in their sixties, and it was really boring there. I somehow convinced the foster Mom to buy an Xbox 360 with the Madden game, and me and the other foster kids were really happy. I shared a room with another foster child, I forget his name, but he was battling cancer. I remember him getting all his hair cut off, he was a really innocent guy, I think he was about fifteen at the time. I don't know what happened to him. There was also Bryan and Colton, they were real brothers, and I was so jealous that their real Dad got them out of CPS. I remember them bragging to me that they were going home to their real family, and that hurt my feelings a lot. Any time you saw other kids getting to go back home it was like a shot to the gut. I was heavy into football at this time, me and next door neighbor would play football every single day. I remember the foster Mom telling me that I wouldn't make it to the NFL, to get a real dream. When she told me that I gave up, I didn't even want to play for the school anymore, I would just play with the neighbors. What kind of person ruins a kid's dream like that?

Mrs. Smith always called me a little shit, and I would talk back to her because she would make me miss the Texans games on Sunday when she forced me to go to church. One time at the church one of the churchgoers "caught" the Holy Ghost and was rolling on the ground, speaking in tongues, and I was laughing so hard because I knew they were full of shit. The foster Dad got mad that I was laughing at the lady rolling on the ground, and the preacher looked so confused as to why I was laughing, so the Dad sent me to the car to wait outside. I used to play basketball at the rec center with the kids in the neighborhood. The basketball had zero grip and The rec center had a big pond next to it so the ball would always bounce into the water, and I would struggle to get it out. Mrs. Smith would try to use talking to Kimberly as a punishment for me. She would not let me talk to Kimberly if I was bad, and I completely lost respect for her when I was behaving well for a long time, and she still never let me talk to Kim. I just gave her hell because all I wanted was to talk to my sister.

CH. 12

There were some families I liked more than others, of course. I really liked the McCullough family. For one thing, they took me and Kimberly together, and that made me happy. We ran away from them, but then they brought us back again. I feel like they truly cared about me, and it was the home I stayed at the longest, from 7th grade to 10th grade. I ran away off and on, but it wasn't because I didn't like them. I really got along with the foster mom's grandson Kobe, he was like my best friend. I ran away from them the last time because they put me in a respite, which is where foster kids go when the family has to go somewhere without them temporarily. It sucked so bad, there was no tv, no entertainment. It was weird to me, the house was kinda sketchy. The African art on the walls gave me haunted vibes, but I thugged it out. When the McCullough family got me I told them "do that again and I will run away." They told me the next time we go out of state you'll come with us, so I was like ok fine, but months passed and they told me I was going to a respite that next week. I jokingly said "don't worry I'll just run away," and they thought I was playing, but that whole week I was preparing to go.

I knew that I was going to run away again, I had a plan and everything. I said I was going to take out the trash and just never came back. I packed my bag and threw it on the roof of my room, I got out and dropped my bag in the bushes in the backyard. Then I came back in and said I was going to go out to take out the trash. They had alarms on the door if it was opened, so I knew that I would need an excuse as to why I was opening a door. I closed the door, left the trash right there, and grabbed my bag. I had called my mom to tell her to come get me, and we went to a hotel and I watched her smoke crack for like 2 days. She was taking her Aunt Marlene's money because Marlene had dementia. I took a picture of all that money and posted it to my Facebook because I knew they were looking on there to figure out where I was, and I put a caption throwing them off: "I'm in Galveston balling, y'all holding me back in cps," but really I was just taking a picture of this money that my mom stole. Then she got paranoid that the cops were gonna get me because she was tweaked out. I told her it was okay, just take me to my dad's. I didn't care what the situation was, I just wanted to be near my family.

She took me to stay with my Dad and the guy he was living with. My brother Brandon was there too, so there wasn't much room. I would sleep on the floor because I didn't have a bed. Every day was the same, I would wake up and watch them watch tv, mostly Judge Judy. I would walk around the woods of the property. My brother had a PlayStation, so we played that a lot. I was in the tenth grade, but I never went back to school. One day I was out with my Dad, he was drunk of course. Brandon was drunk too and had passed out. My Dad decided to push me, I told him to get back but he didn't want to listen, so I beat his ass. He kept saying "I'm sorry, I'm sorry." I was so upset, and it all came tumbling out. "You hit me when I was little, but now I'm older and you can't get away with that shit anymore." I had always wanted to hit him, I thought it would make me feel better, but when I did I felt like a piece of shit. We both apologized, and I left two days later. My mom came and got me, with her aunt Marlene, who my Mom was finessing money out of every day. My mom took all of her money out of the bank; smoking it up, and staying in nice hotels for a long time, it was bad.

CH. 13

After that, I went to stay with my grandparents again. I got a job at the grocery store in the neighborhood, as a cashier and stock boy. I was only sixteen, so I struggled to find a place that would hire me. The paychecks were trash because it wasn't full-time, and my grandparents were asking me to pay rent, so the money didn't last long. Around this time I met a friend and her mom took me into her home and made me legally her foster child. Her name is Mrs. D, and she really took incredible care of me. She called CPS and told them that she had me, and what's crazy is that the caseworker happened to know her. What a wild coincidence. We signed the papers we needed for me to stay there, and CPS was fine with that because they just wanted me to stop running away. If I was happy to stay there, then they were happy.

The idea of me going to Mrs. D only came about because she had an extra ticket for a cruise to the Bahamas, and she invited me along. It was difficult for me to go through because she needed my parents' permission to take me. My grandparents told me that if I went, then they wouldn't want anything to do with me. They were worried that I would be in trouble with CPS as a runaway again, but I told them that it was just a cruise and I would be back in a week. They stuck hard on that no, so Mrs. Devola picked me up after I snuck out the window. We drove out to my Dads trailer at midnight, and we got his signature so that I could go on the cruise. When I got back home to my grandparents' house they realized I had snuck out, and basically told me to leave, so I was homeless at this point. I spent the night at the park, and the next day I tried getting some of my things from my grandparents, but they wouldn't let me. Mrs. Devola bought me all new clothes and everything that I needed for the cruise, and the trip was honestly off the chain. It had really good food and beautiful water. We got back from the cruise and she dropped me off at my grandparents because they had no idea that I had been kicked out.

I tried going inside one more time, but they didn't let me in. I was texting my friend, explaining the situation, and she told her mom. The next thing I know she is picking me up. My mom tried blocking the street to stop her from taking me with them, she was acting crazy. Mrs. Devola swerved around my Mom's van that she was using to block the street. I guess my mom was cracked out at the time, maybe all pilled up, who knows. She never wanted me, but she didn't want me to go with someone who was actually treating me well. Mrs. Devola put me in a home school program, and she paid for my driving school. I was so thankful for her. One day me and my friend got into a car accident, someone T-boned us at a red light, and I got a compressed spine injury. I went to therapy for 5 months, it was extremely challenging, but I recovered. A check came in the mail from the car accident, and I used that to buy a car. Having my own vehicle gave me some independence, and allowed me to get back and forth from work. Growing up the way I did, money was always something I knew I had to worry about.

If it wasn't for her I wouldn't be who I am now. I would have been stuck with my family, turning into someone I didn't want to be. I learned what it was to have a nice family there, to be loved and taken care of. I was there for about 2 years before I got my own place. Once I turned 19, I realized it was time to move on and grow up. I was working at HEB and Walmart and saved up money to move out. I told her it was time for me to move out, and she was really sad and told me that I could stay as long as I liked. It was hard, but it was time. Five months went by, and I got a painter job at a chemical plant, and I was able to get myself a nicer apartment. The transition was hard, I didn't know anything about how to be an adult, but I figured it out and I'm so glad that I was brave enough to take a chance on myself. I'm so thankful for Mrs. Divola, she changed my life.

CH. 14

Although each foster home was different, some things were always the same. Lack of food, not enough food, was pretty common in the foster homes. Too common. A lot of the meals would be really repetitive like I would get sick of eating cereal every morning. I remember asking if I could have a hot breakfast sometimes. The foster parents would get tired of going to the store, if you have six kids at home you can go through a lot of sandwiches in one day, so they would hate it if I asked if I could have two or three. But as we were growing kids, what they were giving us just wasn't enough, I felt like I was always hungry. Kids shouldn't be made to feel guilty for being hungry, they shouldn't have to beg and steal for food. Our most basic needs weren't being met.

One time we were cooking grilled cheese sandwiches, I made the best ones out of the other kids so I was the one doing the cooking. Somehow I started a fire, and I didn't know you couldn't put out a grease fire with water, because no one taught me those kinds of things. Kimberly grabbed the fire extinguisher and put the fire out, but the foster parents were so mad that they said I couldn't cook anymore. I was just a kid, no one taught me how to cook, I was doing the best I could. A couple of times I put ramen noodles in the microwave and forgot the water, so it started smoking. If someone would have taken the time to just show me, they could have avoided these moments, but that was not something that they cared to do. At most of the homes you weren't allowed to be in the kitchen without permission, you had to ask. At one home they were going to put a lock on the fridge and cabinets so that we couldn't get any food unless they gave it to us, they had a lock on the air conditioner too so we couldn't turn up the air. That is why it sometimes felt like we were in jail, we weren't allowed to do basic things in the home.

When you are in a foster home that has biological kids, obviously you are treated differently. When they would take their kids places, I would ask if I could go. They would always say no. Even if it was just to go to Walmart or Kroger, just to get out of the house. Sometimes they would come back with Wing Stop, and I'm home eating bologna sandwiches. It was especially hard with gifts, I understand how it's expensive, not everyone gets a PlayStation. But my foster parents didn't even try to make things a little more even for us. As a kid it just all seems so unfair. One year I got a football, a watch, and socks from CPS. I was upset because the other kids got much nicer presents. A foster mom's grandson was laughing at me, telling me that my Mom didn't love me. It stuck with me forever. He was 8 and I was 14, rubbing it in, just making me feel terrible. I know it's just kids being jerks, but sometimes those moments stay fixed in your mind, and you never really get over that. That's why teaching your kids to be kind is so important, you never know the scar you are leaving.

I never really dated much, I had big trust issues because of the way I was raised, imagine adding a broken heart to everything else. I had so much on my mind, my family, it was never really what I was thinking about. There were times that it came up, of course, it just never got serious until I was older. The first time I ever had contact with a girl was in 6th grade science class and she really liked me. One day she came and grabbed my hand, she made me squeeze her breast. I was really shy, but nothing really happened after that.

In a foster home, I kissed this girl like 3 times, nothing serious. It was all mostly curiosity. When I was at Another foster home, her cousin brought her daughter over, she was like 3 years older than me. She came in and laid down next to me, was kinda flirting with me and grabbing up on me, but nothing happened. It was a one-time thing because I never showed interest back. This is the kind of thing most people don't even think about, how growing up in the system affects every part of your life, even the idea of romance is tainted.

Money was always something I wanted so that I could buy things for myself, but as a kid, there aren't many ways to make that happen. I used to sell candy at school, and it was straight profit because I would steal the candy from the dollar store. The foster parents would question me, how could I afford to get myself a phone? One time I bought an Amazon tablet online and traded it for an iPhone with a kid at school. One of the foster brothers caught on to my candy business, but he got caught stealing, so then they knew what we were doing. I never got caught though, so I was like "I don't know what you are talking about." It was such an easy hussle at school, the kids would ask each other, where did you get that candy from, and I'd sell out. I would also sell those little paper spinners, kids loved those at school. I would only make like $5, but still, it was money coming in.

The first job I had was at the Smith's foster home, they had a lawnmower just sitting in the back, so I asked if I could use it. I knocked on doors and offered to do the front and back for $10. I would do six or seven houses in a row, so it added up. My shoes would be green, and I would be exhausted, but I was paid. My first real job was at the grocery store around the corner from my grandparents. I was stocking, grabbing carts, and I was a cashier. I was always looking for a way to make money so that I could buy better shoes and nicer clothes. I was bullied over my

Walmart clothes, especially if I was the only white boy at school. You have to know how to dress, and how to roast kids back. One kid was talking shit about my shoes, and I said "you built like a wet cigarette, go sit your kids' cuisine eating ass down." Everyone ate that shit up, so no one was fucking with me about my Walmart shoes. They would call me Peter Parker, but that was ok, I'll take that over white boy.

CH. 15

There was a time in high school when I took this kid's spot on the team, so the kid Levi wanted to fight me. The other kids would tease him, the only white boy took your spot, you trash. It was only JV, but I was proud of myself. I was walking by to get to my side of the field, and the other coach was joking around, "let's see if this white boy can catch this pass since he can't do it." There was a play where the varsity wide receiver kept dropping the ball, or couldn't beat his man on defense. The coach saw me, the only white boy on the team, I was running back to my side of the field after getting some water. He said, hey come here, run a streak. If you catch the ball you're going to take his spot. I went to the huddle and the quarterback told me exactly where the ball would fall down, so after I beat my man and got up that sideline, the ball was placed perfectly into double coverage. I came down with the ball and the coaches couldn't believe it, the team was going crazy, and I got up from the ground kind of surprised that I caught it. That was a really funny moment for me because people called me Peter Parker or horsepower just because of that one play at practice. Man, I felt like the shit.

The hard thing about being in foster care and playing sports would be those games where I would look up at the stands and realize that there was no one there to watch me. I loved the game, but it would have been so much better knowing I had someone cheering me on, supporting me, just someone to be proud of me. I did meet one of my best friends at this time though, Raymond. He said that he befriended me because he thought I would be a school shooter because I was the only white boy at the school, and he knew his chances to survive were better if we were friends. I knew we would be good friends because he had a dark sense of humor just like me. It was of course a horrible joke, but we were kids just trying to connect, using humor to deal. It really helped to have a good friend. I did have a lot of fun playing football in high school though, it gave me direction and something to do. I was good at it too, so it helped my self-esteem. They wanted me to run track over there, but I didn't want to do it. Football was the main way I made friends, it helped me to let the anger out, hitting and getting hit cleared my head. Although I didn't want to run track for school, I did like to run for myself. I would run until I felt pain in my legs, and I would keep running, I didn't care. For me it was what I did anytime I was feeling sad or angry, I would blast my music so loud that I didn't have to think, and just run.

I never had money to buy the right equipment I needed for

football, so I had to make do. At school, there was another kid, and he let me have his baseball cleats because he was moving away. They were ugly and used, but they were mine. The school supplied the shoulder pads, and man those fuckers looked old, but my foster parents were going to buy new ones for me. I didn't have the right kind of helmet, each position had different face masks on their helmet. I was playing safety, so I needed a little mask, but that wasn't the one they gave me. I just had to use what they had, the old equipment. Everything was out of place, I looked ridiculous. The only thing new that I had was the uniform because we had just got them. I don't have a picture of me in the uniform because there was no one there to take a picture. The game I had one of my best plays ever creating a fumble at the 1-yard line, no one was there to see it. I remember sitting there after making the play looking at the stands seeing people so happy and excited it became a blur. I would tell my sister Shannon that she could come and watch me play, and she would say she would come, but they never showed up. They didn't let Kimberly come to my games, I wished we were at the same high school so that she could watch me play.

One time when Kimberly and I were at the same school, there was a girl in school who was trying to fight me in the classroom, and I was running from her telling her "I can't hit you, you are a girl, but hold on a second I got someone for you." The bell rang, perfect timing, and I ran out of

class straight to Kimberly's classroom and told her a girl
was trying to fight me. Kimberly drug her down that
hallway. She always had my back like that. She is the person
who taught me how to be strong, she showed me what to,
and not, to do. She is the reason I'm not scared of
monsters. She spent hours teaching me how to cuss in the
back of the school bus. She was my everything.

CH. 16

I had a lot of caseworkers over the years, but my favorite one was Jennifer Taylor. She wore her hair in a black and blonde weave, and I remember she had a big gap in her teeth. She was really nice, she would always pay for us to get something out of the vending machine. She was really trying hard not to split me and Kimberly up, she knew how much we wanted to stay together. She would ask questions and try to find solutions for us. We always wanted to talk to our mom, and she would let us use her cell phone really quickly. She was the one that announced when my Dad lost his rights, and she told us that this would actually be our last visit. I think he knew before the visit. I cried all through the rest of the visit. She was with me for three or four years before she moved back to Mississippi. After that, I bounced around a lot of case workers, a couple weeks with one and then a different person. I would always ask, when can I see my mom, and they would stop me and say, "wait first we need to catch up on you." I would have to tell them the same things over and over again, the new caseworkers didn't always get the notes from the last one, so it was the same things over and over.

One case worker I had, her name was Melinda, she was rude. I didn't respect her at all. The very first time I ran away was from her. She was too straightforward, this is the law, this is what is going to happen. I was a little kid, I didn't want to hear that, I needed someone who could be more understanding. Kids don't care about the law, they don't know what all that means, they just want to see their Mom. She didn't try, she wasn't kind, I didn't matter to her. Mark Waters, the one who was friends with Mrs. Devola, he was cool. He wore his Jordans, he talked to me about video games and football, he tried to relate to me. Kids aren't stupid, they can tell when you are trying, when you care. He just didn't want me to run away anymore, he would tell me "we want to know where you are, that you are safe." I believed him when he said that, he just needed to know that I was okay and they would leave me alone. The thing is, being in foster care is hard enough, if you don't have a good caseworker it makes things even tougher. These kids don't need that.

A lot of the other kids that leave the system, you see them going down the wrong path, and I knew that I didn't want to do the same. I saw my sister fall into a life of drugs and adversity when she aged out of CPS, and that is pretty common. There were big gaps in my life that I wasn't around her because CPS wouldn't let me. They wouldn't even let me and Kimberly talk because they were afraid we would plan to run away if we talked. We had phone calls monitored by the foster parents for short periods of time. I just never got interested in that lifestyle of drugs and alcohol because I had already seen what it does to people. My Mom was smoking crack, and my dad was drinking, I got this fear of trying drugs and alcohol. I was scared to find comfort in them, I didn't want to be like my parents, so I looked down on all of it. That is one good thing that came from my experiences, I learned from the mistakes of others, and it probably saved me from getting into trouble when I was older.

When I got my first real job with a nice paycheck, and I finally got my own place, I was very excited about being independent for the first time. I played a lot of video games, worked, and ate a bunch of trash. I was living the teenage life, but I was taking care of myself, on my own terms. Once I got the job that I have now, a really good job, I pulled up to my grandparents' house in my own car, in my work uniform, and damn that felt good. I was proud of myself, and what I had accomplished. Shannon told them that I was on drugs, that I was an alcoholic, a lot of stuff that wasn't true. I don't know if she was jealous that I had decided to make something of myself, to not settle for the life that she had chosen, but they were proud of me.

CH. 17

As difficult as my childhood was, everything that I went through, the worst moment of my life was when Kimberly died. It was a car accident, she lost control of the vehicle, it went through a gate and hit a parked car. That other car was pushed through another gate, that's how much force there was. The worst part was that her boys were in the back seat. They were okay, but they had to witness everything. The boys told me, "I kept trying to wake Kimberly up." They called grandma Mom because Kimberly always called Carol Mom. Kids are funny like that, they pick up on what the others around them do, so that was normal for them.

At the funeral home, they asked me if I wanted to see the body, but they warned me it was graphic. I said no, that's not how I wanted to remember her. She was so beautiful, and that is how she will stay in my mind. They did the viewing of the body outside in front of the building, my Dad and my other siblings went to look. My dad took a picture of her when he viewed her. Then at the memorial on June 19th, he pulled his phone out, and it took me a few seconds to realize it was Kimberly's' body that he was showing me. I looked at him and started cursing "what's wrong with you, you don't do that." He was showing everybody. He kept saying " I just wanted to see how people reacted if they really loved her." I couldn't sleep for days, I kept seeing her face all bruised and broken. That was such a cruel thing to do, I was very clear that I didn't want to see her like that. And to parade her picture around like that was so crass, so inappropriate.

The day after her car accident, May 29th, I stayed there with the kids all day, from 8am till 11pm. They were so confused, they kept saying "Kimberly died," but then they would ask for her. Trying to process something like that is hard for anyone, but at that age, it's just so overwhelming. I remember being in that horrible accident when I was a kid, and knowing that things could have turned out so much worse. Now my nephews were in the same situation, but with an entirely different outcome. I knew that this was going to be one of those events that shaped everyone's future, there would be a before and after this day. Days later I went to Kimberly's apartment to gather some sentimental items. The place was trashed and they stole her tv and computer. Someone had slashed her clothes, they had ripped up a bible all over the apartment. The only thing they left was a black dress hanging up in the closet, the same dress that she wore to our grandfather's funeral. I took the dress, and I took the Marilyn Monroe pics down that she loved and handed them out to the family. I got her phone from her car because I knew her pictures and contacts were in it. I have her bracelet and necklace that she was wearing when she died, I wear them all the time. I haven't seen my dad since Kimberly's funeral, we had Kimberly cremated, I need to get her ashes from him. It took me some time, but I learned that you can't help someone who doesn't need to be helped.

CH. 18

My Dad had his rights terminated in February of 2010, and my Mom's visitations were terminated by the judge in June of 2010. I always felt hurt about it, I still do. If you can't go to court dates or pass drug tests to try and get your children back, children who are crying for you, I just have no words. It made it worse because she would lie, tell me everything will be fine, "I'm going to get you back", and then turn around and not go to her court dates. Sometimes she wouldn't even show up to CPS visits when she could have. I've always had this lost and scared feeling in my body, ever since I can remember, like my parents just threw me away. It made me feel like I wasn't important enough for them to make the effort, I didn't mean enough to them for them to change their lives to get us back. Your parents are supposed to love you, and be willing to do anything to keep you safe, but that isn't always true.

I used to have Cherophobia when I was little, it used to make me cry at the strangest things. As an adult I understand it was a trauma response, but as a kid, you don't know why you feel the way you do. I was just scared all of the time. When something good happened to me I just knew something bad was going to follow. One day I got an attitude with myself about it. I told myself "don't be scared" basically, just facing the fear in my own head, and eventually I got over it. I didn't want to be paralyzed by this fear all of my life, not allowing myself to appreciate the good moments while I was in them. Enough had been taken from me, I didn't need to steal my own joy.

Before Kimberly died, Shannon was in jail around March/April for assault. Kimberly did not want her seven kids to go into foster care, so she took the kids in. Shannon got out on the day that Kimberly died, and they fought because Kimberly didn't take the pets too. Shannon started to threaten to call CPS on her. I read the text messages of them fighting, can you imagine that being the last thing you said to your sister? I had Kimberly's phone, and it kept going off as the news of what happened spread, and it went off all night, so I had to turn it off. I stupidly gave all of her things to my mom, including the phone. I tried to get it back, to get the pictures off it for her kids. My Mom said she lost it, and I went off on her. That's worth more than I could ever make!

I'm not on speaking terms with my mother or my sister, especially after everything that happened around

Kimberly's death. I can't bring myself to care when they have proven how much they don't. As much as I hoped they would change, would make up for everything that happened, I don't think they ever will. Sometimes you just have to accept that people are who they are, and it is up to you to decide if you want to continue to be exposed to that negativity and hatefulness. When Kimberly died, I lost a part of myself, and the last real family I had. It's a different type of pain I'm experiencing because now that Kimberly is gone, I feel truly alone. I'm not really on speaking terms with any blood family. It's a terrible thing to say, but I am at the point in my life where I can recognize that blood doesn't always mean that people want the best for you and that they care as they should.

My Uncle James is paralyzed, he was going to go into a care facility, and he didn't want to lose what he put into his house. He tried to sell me his house because he needed someone that could take care of it. I told him that I couldn't afford it, but he said to just pay him what I could and he would pay the rest. When Shannon heard about it for some unknown reason. She tells him "don't let him have it. I have 6 kids, I can pay you the money. If you give it to him he will have parties or sell it." So my uncle tells me he talked to Shannon, and "she told me alot about you. I know what your intentions are. I am going to keep the house." I was so hurt that he would believe all those lies about me, so I decided to just let him keep sitting there in his negative energy and "walk away." I felt like shit saying that, but I was tired of people believing what they heard about me. I work hard, I don't do drugs or drink, I have not asked for anyone to help me out, and now you believe all this shit. Kimberly was the only one speaking good on my name, because she was the only person I talked to who really knew me. They were not a part of my life. But I knew Kimberly, and she knew me.

Me and my uncle used to talk via email, talking about the Texans. I even offered to come and watch the game at his place since he was not getting around well. I offered to bring the pizza, just trying to build the relationship, but something would always come up. He didn't want me to go to my grandfather's funeral. I had to find out the time and place myself, and I sat at the back alone during the funeral. I walked up to the front, crying at the coffin, and walked back to my seat, the only one crying in the whole room was me and Kimberly. They were focused on the money that they were about to get, but I didn't care, I was just sad to know that my grandfather was gone. When my grandma died, he pointed to their shared tombstone and said "there's where I'm going to be." They played taps, there were only a few people there, and they fired the guns into the air. I remember Kimberly wearing that black dress when she leaned over the coffin, and that was the only thing left hanging in her closet when her place got ransacked.

Once my grandfather died, I felt like I had a male role model. I realized that I mirrored him a lot. My grandfather wrote a book when he was in the army, and I really wanted to read it, get an idea of what he was like then. He got shot in the shoulder and had a big dent in his arm. He would tell me war stories about being in Germany, and I think it changed him. The book went to his son, but he wouldn't let me get a copy. I just wanted to get to know my grandfather more, but they thought I would sell it. I told them, I'll come to you and you can read it to me, I just want to hear it. He had a purple heart, war medals, he stood for all of the things that mattered. He was polite to women, a hard worker, a genuinely good man. The kind of man that I want to be.

CH. 19

Growing up in the system, I get asked a lot about my experiences, and how things could be done better. I think this is such an important question because those kids need more than they are getting right now. People need to understand that if you work with kids, especially CPS, it needs to be more than just a job. And if you have good people that work for you, treat them right, pay them more, make sure they know that they matter. I'm an adult, and I still remember the impact that a good social worker can make. Kids aren't stupid, they can tell if you really care about them, and they really need someone to care.

When they do home visits, inspections to make sure that the kids are treated well, it was scheduled. That means that the foster parents could make sure that everything looked nice, and they would tell us to get cleaned up and put on a nice face. These visits need to be impromptu so that you can see what the home is really like. They need to be more strict on the parents and believe the kids if they tell you something. If I tell you that I am going to bed hungry, and the foster parents say "He is just kidding", why don't you believe me? We stole food from the fridge in the middle of the night and dropped the trash in a hole that someone punched into the wall so we wouldn't get in trouble. We went to bed hungry a lot, we were growing, and we needed more than we were getting. I wouldn't sleep well because I was hungry. I know these parents were getting food stamps, so why weren't we eating? This shouldn't be happening.

It's important to find the balance between the kids and the foster parents. They would say "he needs medicine, he's sad all the time." Yeah, I am sad, because I don't have all the things I'm used to, I miss my family. I have to fight with a foster brother I'm stuck in a room with. Don't try to put me on medication, try to understand that my life has been turned upside down. I can't see my family, it's like I'm in jail, so yeah I'm sad. I felt like I was locked up in jail at times because everything we did was restricted. I wasn't allowed to do things that I used to do, I had to deal with rules I wasn't used to, I had to stay in the house most of the time. No kid is going to thrive in conditions like that. They have already taken you away from everything and everyone you have ever known, they should be going out of their way to try and make it as easy on you as possible. There was an extreme lack of empathy, of understanding.

They would give us clothing vouchers twice a year, every six months. The vouchers were good for Walmart or Target, we would get $120, and that could only be used on clothing. That may seem like a lot of money, but that had to cover everything; shoes, socks, belts, underwear, and clothes. I got bullied at school for wearing those shoes, everyone else had the nice name-brand ones and I was the foster kid with the cheap shoes. Why aren't we donating clothes to these kids? There are huge clothing and shoe companies that could step up and set up a program for these kids, and write it off as a donation. Imagine the difference that it would make, instead of feeling ashamed because you are getting teased for what you are wearing, you would be proud to show up to school wearing the same nice clothes as everyone else. Things were hard enough, we got bullied for being foster kids, for going to school dirty, now add on to that being bullied for what we were wearing. Sometimes we would borrow each other's clothes so that we weren't wearing the same shirt every day. At least that way we could vary our wardrobe a bit, we wouldn't look so weird for only having three shirts. We would write our initials on the tag on the inside so we knew who it belonged to.

Another issue is that all of the benefits expire. There is no long-term counseling available, no assistance programs aimed at teaching you how to be an adult. These kids need long-term help, long term benefits to help deal with the lasting trauma that exists. Think about war vets, they have PTSD support, why don't we do that for kids that are the result of the system. We are drafted into that life, it's not our choice, but we deal with the aftermath forever. You have to deal with not only the present but what future that present is creating. People take for granted that they have a support system, a family to help them out if they get into a position and they need a hand. Who is my person? There is no safety net, so every chance I take has to be calculated. I have to look out for myself.

There are actually statistics on this, they track how many ex-foster kids go to college, or start their own businesses compared to their peers. The numbers are drastically skewed. You are less likely to take a chance on something if you know you don't have anyone backing you up. If I can't pay my rent, I can't go and move back in with my parents until I get on my feet again. And simple things like the holidays when you don't have family, or moments of accomplishments when there is no one to share that with. There are so many areas of your life that are affected by growing up in the system, it is like a shadow cast over everything.

Most importantly, there needs to be an actual life skills class. How do you find a place to live, how do you get all of your utilities turned on, how do you get yourself set up? We need classes that teach kids how to cook, how to wash their own clothes, how to do their taxes. Basic things like knowing how often to get your car's oil changed, or how to grocery shop on a budget, no one thinks to teach kids this when they age out of the system. We don't have a family to teach us these basic life skills, no one to explain all of the everyday details of being an adult on your own. I remember having anxiety about things as simple as making a doctor's appointment because the insurance was so confusing, and I didn't know the answers to all of the questions they were asking. These kids need to be set up to succeed, they need to feel confident in their ability to take care of themselves.

CONCLUSION

Kimberly always used to tell me to keep my head up, only the strong survive the bullshit. That is what I do for her, for myself, and for all the other kids still in the system. It amazes me when I see how strong these kids are, they are doing their best to get through a hard situation. I see so much of myself in them. They are proof that no matter what you go through, there is always a chance to do better, to be better. Some of them might not get that chance until they are out, but some get lucky and find an adult who genuinely wants to help. That's all it takes, one person to make a difference in these kids' lives.

That is what I want people to understand, these kids need more help than we are giving them. We simply aren't doing enough. If we want them to survive the system without it completely breaking their spirits, breaking their hearts, they need more support. I wish I could go back in time and be that person for Kimberly and I, but the best I can do is shine a light on the foster system, tell the truth about my experience, and hope it makes a difference to someone.

After everything, I am proud of the man I am today, and I know that Kimberly would be proud of me too. I want people to see that although many kids age out, or run away, and get caught up in the dark side of life, that it doesn't have to go that way. It is possible to create a happy and healthy life, but it would be so much easier if we gave them the tools for success. We need to do a better job of taking care of these kids while they are in the system and making sure that they are ready for life when they leave it.

There are always going to be storms in life, but if you know how to use your umbrella to stay dry, things are going to be much easier. If you can take that lesson, and show someone else how to use their own, teach them that they don't have to brave the rain alone, even better.